Life and Survival
THE KESTREL

Nicolas Van Ingen and
Jean-François Hellio

FRANKLIN WATTS
in association with
TWO-CAN

In the heart of the country...

In this corner of the countryside, the lanes are lined with hedges. A carpet of white daisies covers the middle of a field where cows are grazing. A lark calls high in the sky. In the oak and chestnut trees, robins and chaffinches challenge each other in loud voices. A butterfly tries vainly to escape from a hungry hedge sparrow.

And there, motionless on a rock, a small, tawny bird of prey is on the lookout. From time to time, his eyes flicker. This is the kestrel's territory. He surveys his surroundings.

Look out for kestrels among the hedges. They can usually be spotted in farmland areas which have not yet been destroyed by modern agriculture or chemicals.

The hunter's weapons

Perched on the rock, the kestrel looks very small. He is only 35 cm high, which is much smaller than most birds of prey. The buzzard is four times bigger than the kestrel, as is its cousin, the fearsome peregrine falcon.

Weapon number 1: keen sight. The kestrel can spot the movement of a tiny vole more than 100 m away.

But the little kestrel is an excellent hunter. Each morning before setting off to hunt, he checks his armour. Above all, his plumage must be impeccable. If it is dirty or in bad condition, he cannot fly or attack his prey with his usual flair and agility. Carefully, the kestrel smoothes his feathers with his beak, paying particular attention to the long wing and tail feathers. These feathers ensure the speed and precision of his flight.

Weapon number 3: sharp claws. Three toes in front and one behind seize the prey like a pincer. The victim is cut and torn by this deadly grip.

Weapon number 2: pointed beak. This is armed with a small tooth so that he can kill his prey with one blow.

Weapon number 4: hovering flight. The kestrel is a specialist at hovering in the air while he searches for his prey.

A swooping attack

Now the kestrel is ready for the hunt. He takes off, then hangs motionless in the air, playing with the wind. He spreads out his tail feathers like a fan, and flaps his wings rapidly. His head is perfectly still, eyes fixed on the ground. He can spot the tiniest quiver in the grass, 30 metres below.

The kestrel hovers in the sky, looking for food.

Beneath the ground is a maze of tunnels made by voles, the kestrel's prey. Any vole who ventures out had better take care.

Suddenly, something moves: it is a small rodent.

The kestrel draws back his wings and drops towards the ground. Suspecting nothing, the vole continues to nibble. He thinks he is safely hidden in the grass. Suddenly the kestrel swoops down head first towards his prey. At the last moment, he turns around, spreads his wings and seizes the vole in his claws. One peck of the kestrel's sharp beak and it's the end for the poor vole.

At the end of some summers, voles breed very rapidly. There may be thousands of them in one small area.

By the time the vole notices this menacing shadow...

...it is already too late.

Make way for the night hunters!

The kestrel usually eats three or four voles a day. When there are lots of voles about, half an hour of hunting is enough to find all the food he needs. But when food is scarce, the kestrel flies for hours on an empty stomach, catching only a few insects. If it rains too much, he will find nothing to eat at all.

If there are not many trees about the kestrel will perch on whatever he finds.

There is no hunting when night falls.

Slowly, sounds begin to die out. Only the singing of the blackbirds breaks the silence. An owl's shadow glides over a hedge. A weasel rustles in the grass. It's their turn now to go hunting. The kestrel has left them the night shift. He is settled on his night perch, sheltered from the wind, rain and prowling stone martens. In the distance, a tawny owl hoots. The kestrel is sleeping, with his head tucked under his wing.

Kestrels often gather in small groups to sleep in the same tree. Others prefer to spend the night alone.

Love at first sight

In the morning, the kestrel returns to his usual post. But what a surprise, another kestrel is already there! It is a female. The male, furious at first, whirls around making small cries. How dare this intruder come into his territory.

But his unfriendliness soon turns into a mating game. Flapping his wings, he flies up in the air and pretends to swoop down on the female. He flies in circles, moving only the ends of his tail feathers. The female seems to be interested...

He courts her for several days, bringing her small rodents as gifts. Their pairing up is decided at least for the season.

Couples form at the beginning of spring. They do not mind other couples in their hunting territory. They will only defend the immediate area around their nest.

It is easy to tell the kestrels apart. The female's head is the same tawny colour as the rest of her body. Her tail is lined with black stripes.

The male is more colourful. The feathers on his head are blue-grey. His tail is also grey, with one thick black stripe at the end.

This valley would be dangerous. The neighbours are not very friendly! Owls and peregrine falcons living here often eat kestrels.

This solitary tree is perfect.
Too bad a crow is already living there.
Maybe next year...

Finding a nest is the male's job.
And it's not easy!

Searching for a nest

The male explores the area, looking for a place to nest. Perhaps on this cliff there is a small crevice sheltered from the rain. That would suit him perfectly.

Most birds of prey are very fussy about their nests, but the kestrel would be happy to use an old crow's nest, a hole in the wall, the top of an electricity pole or a place under a bridge. Some even nest on the ground in sand dunes. Kestrels never build their own nests, not even bringing a few twigs to make them comfortable.

This spot looks quiet. But it's too late. An owl has already laid her eggs here.

17

Patience, patience!

Finally, the female makes her decision. She settles in an old crow's nest at the top of a pine tree. It is very well placed, right in the middle of their hunting ground. Here, the two kestrels can spot crows and magpies from far away and will attack them if they come too close.

The eggs are laid over two or three days. There are usually between three and seven of them. Sometimes two kestrels lay in the same nest, but this is rare.

The female starts to sit on her eggs before she has laid all of them. This is why the babies are not all born on the same day.

At last, in June the eggs are laid. The female hardly ever leaves the nest now. The male brings her food regularly. Cooing excitedly, she takes the vole he has brought her, and goes off a little way to eat it. Meanwhile, the male takes care of the eggs. In under half an hour, the female is back.

After 25 days, the female does not leave the nest at all, not even to eat. Hatching time is not far off and she must not miss the moment of birth!

Watch out! This magpie would not hesitate to gobble up an egg or two.

The birth

The first baby broke out of his shell in the night. He is already interested in everything around him. Nodding his head, he follows the path of a fly. It is very hot. Luckily his mother is here to shade him with her protective wings.

In a few days the family is complete. Now the struggle to survive begins. The baby who chirps the loudest will be served first. And if there is not enough food for everyone, too bad!

Two eggs out of the batch have not hatched. Perhaps they were not fertilised or were not able to withstand the change in temperature. Unfortunately, this happens quite often. Anyway, the parents would have trouble filling six hungry mouths.

For the first two weeks, the female almost never leaves the nest. She spends all her time looking after her chicks.

At birth, the babies are covered in white down. They weigh 15 grams.

The first layer of down is replaced in the second week by a pinky grey down. The feathers start to appear after the twentieth day. When the babies are a month old they have all their feathers.

The male has just brought home some food. It is always the female who cuts it up and feeds the babies.

Beware of the kestrel

Two weeks later, the fragile chicks have become strong and eager for food. The male's hunting does not bring enough food, so the female must join him.

Anything will do: voles, fieldmice, grasshoppers, lizards, crickets, cockchafers, shrews, moles, earthworms and small birds. Even bats should watch out. A hunting bird will attack anything that moves. One after the other, twenty times a day, the male and the female bring their prey to the nest. When they arrive, the young kestrels start to cry and hop about. They grab the prey, trying to pull it to pieces by themselves.

The chicks are usually born at a time when there is a lot of prey about. When a spring is cold and there is a lot of rain, it is very difficult to feed the hungry chicks.

In Europe, 80% of a kestrel's prey are voles or fieldmice. In southern countries, they eat mostly lizards.

Like all hunting animals, the kestrel does not succeed in every attack.
Often, he has to give up having caught nothing.

23

The adventurers

After a month, the baby kestrels venture to the edge of the nest. They flap their wings frantically. Soon they are hopping from one branch to another, catching one another if they slip.

The young birds learn to fly without even thinking about it. But learning to hunt is much more difficult. Luckily, their parents are sitll here to bring them fresh meat.

A large number of kestrels die during their first year. Six out of ten will not live to see the following spring. Only the strongest live eight or nine years. The longest a kestrel has been known to live is 16 years.

Six eggs were laid, four chicks were born and now there are only two. The others have died and been eaten by the older birds.

By August, the young kestrels can fend for themselves. They take off to explore the world. Some settle nearby while others fly hundreds of kilometres to find new territories.

Before winter, young and adult birds migrate. The more adventurous fly far, crossing mountains, seas and deserts to hotter climates. Others only go a little way, in spite of the winter cold.

Always about

The kestrel is the most common bird of prey seen in the day time. Farmers like kestrels because they keep fields clear of voles and fieldmice. However, although kestrels are now protected by law, they too often fall victim to man's stupidity.

In the city where there are no voles, the kestrel eats sparrows.

These young kestrels are ready for take off.

Hunting pests

Many kestrels have been killed by people who intended to get rid of crows, magpies and other so-called pests. Every year in May and June, hunters shoot at magpies' and crows' nests, not knowing that kestrels also use them for nesting. It was only in 1989 that this dangerous and senseless practice was banned too.

Shot and poisoned

Although the law protects kestrels, many of them are still shot every year by uncaring hunters. Animal shelters that look after injured birds receive 150 to 200 a year. Out of these, a third have been electrocuted or poisoned with pesticides. As a hunter at the end of the food chain the kestrel takes in a concentrated amount of pesticides which have been absorbed by all its prey.

Help an injured kestrel

Wrap the bird in thick cloth before you handle it. Make sure you cover its sharp beak and claws. Put it in a box with breathing holes punched in the top.
Do not disturb it. Birds of prey are afraid of people and experience great stress when captured. Then telephone the RSPB who will tell you where to find their nearest centre. There, the bird will be in good hands.

No fences in sight. Never mind! This statue's finger makes a very good perch!

In the cities

Today kestrels can be found everywhere: in the countryside, on the edge of motorways, on hilltops and on cliffs at the seaside. Braving pollution, they even settle in large cities, nesting in church towers and sometimes in skyscrapers!

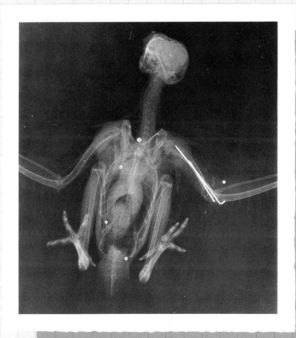

This kestrel was injured by five shots. It now has a pin in its broken wing.

Other falcons

The kestrel is part of the falcon family. Falcons are birds of prey that hunt in the day. They only hunt living animals. They are recognisable by their tapering wings and narrow tail. They flap their wings very rapidly. These characteristics enable them to accelerate fast and fly with spectacular agility. Unlike birds of prey that depend on rising air currents, the falcon can fly in any weather, thanks to a powerful set of muscles. Female falcons are much bigger than males, but the males are more colourful. No falcon builds its own nest. There are big falcons and small falcons, all of them easy to recognise...

▲
The *hobby* looks like a miniature peregrine falcon and is a great acrobat. With its long, pointed wings it flies rather like a swift. It catches small birds and insects in mid-flight with incredible ease and eats them in the air. It is a migrating bird that is only seen in Europe from April to September.

The *peregrine falcon* is one of the biggest falcons in Europe. It is a fearsome hunter and catches its prey in swoops of up to 400 km an hour. It lives mostly on cliffs as does its enemy the great horned owl. In winter they can be found everywhere. Two things have made life difficult for the peregrine falcon: a pesticide called DDT which was used in farming and which damaged their eggs; and the poaching of their babies for falconry. Luckily, thanks to the efforts of certain organisations, both of these problems are less widespread than they used to be. ▶

◀ The *falconet* looks very like the kestrel, but it is smaller and has markings on its back. It is an expert at hunting insects such as crickets, grasshoppers, locusts and centipedes. Unfortunately, nowadays these birds have almost disappeared.

INDEX

First published in this edition in 1991 by
Franklin Watts
96 Leonard Street
London EC2A 4RH

French edition © Editions Milan 1990, 300 rue Léon Joulin 31101, Cedex 100, France
English edition © Two-Can Publishing Ltd 1991, 27 Cowper Street, London EC2A 4AP
English translation by Melanie Brumberg

A CIP cataloguing record for this book is available from the British Library
ISBN 0-7496-0721-1

Printed in Belgium by Casterman, SA

Photographs © N. Van Ingen and J-F Hellio except
BIOS: A. Fatras p.28 R. Seitre p.29 (top)
Alain DALMOLIN: p.27 (bottom)